SNATCHING AT BUBBLES

SNATCHING AT BUBBLES

Tony Weston

WINWALOE

Published 2001 by
WINWALOE
Bundles Barn
Nuthampstead
Royston
SG8 8LS

ISBN 0 9530828 2 2

British Library Cataloguing-in-publication Data.
A catalogue record for this book is available
from the British Library.

Printed in Great Britain by
The Burlington Press,
Foxton, Cambridge, CB2 6SW

Grateful thanks to Bundle
for all that proof-reading
and strict inspiration

and to my brother Peter
for the Author's Photo.

Acknowledgement is due to John Wakeman,
the Editor of the SHOp,
who first published 1st January 2000

Cover : Bundle on the phone—
by the author

For Sophie

Contents

It is

It is snatching at bubbles.

It is pinning the wind on a wet finger.

It is never quite knowing the steps of the dance
            you might have been asked to—

Surprised

Surprised by your voice on the telephone,
though I sit anxiously waiting your call
with you ensconced so real in my head,
you sudden and close, yet sounding so far,
poor fool I sit stunned, brain-dead,
words stilted, failing to flow.
Words stilted, failing to flow,
backed-up in the silt of familiar years,
the winter debris, the summer drought,
the worn stone parchment of our days?
Now, somewhere beneath, in bedrock rises
the spring of love, the well of tears
that swells my sides and breaks
to unlooked laughter, spills
ridiculous salt water down my face
and sweeps me, feet gone under, out to sea—

Hello? you say – *Love, are you there? It's me.*

Had I full Summer

Had I full summer in my hand
I would bestow it not on flowers,
nor would I let its golden hours
lie in the aching land,
but I would set it in your hair
and worship there.

A simple question

Are you happy?
Hand on your heart:
is the beat
like the skip
of children's feet?

Hand on your heart, now,
are you sad?
Is it the tread
of all who despaired
and are dead?

Open your eyes.
Is it bright as waking
to a Summer's day --
or has staring
at yesterday
and tomorrow
taken the moment's
colours away?

Warm libation for Mr. Inch
August 18th 1970

You died
as we were eating
jelly and blancmange.

They let the trolley
with the tea
come past,
before the screens

across the passage
where, revived,
you walked
four nights ago,

obscured our line of sight.

They let the trolley past—
pots of tea
aren't made to last.

No crumbs

She talks in anger
and in hurt,
this girl of eighty,
eloquent of hand,
her head askance,

The glances flit between us.

She sits, hand to her mouth,
dead still, though,
in her rubbed-thin
temple beats
the unrelinquishable drum.

As sparrows, glances flit between us.

She pats the space beside.
The fool is dead.
The thanks he had
a square peg
with a piece across.

The sparrows hop and dance between us.

They burned him up,
left me the flowers,
a house stuffed full
of drawers of vests,
drawers of socks,
all these bloody photographs.

The sparrows skip between our feet.

They leave no crumbs,
the little buggers
leave no crumbs.
She looks me in the eye
and grins . . .

Death/commute life
1

Soft
hang of bacon on the air
like the bad breath of love
and, out of the sheets,
in the grey, damp street,
his grey heart breaking,
he walks
with his eyes half-shut
and his dreams half-open.

> I walk like a man
> from the bed of the sea
> and the stones I climb
> cry after me,
> salt-tongue in my throat,
> salt-hand at my knee,
> clutching.

Silver the track
kerbing the sun,
singing the train
that he must catch,
for which he runs;

> while something missed
> moves in my brain,
> here, and here,
> pulls both ways,
> here, by the bucket
> on the wall,
> the waiting day
> slides wide its jaws.

Stand clear the doors.

Lucky the man
finding it empty,
the corner seat,
the neat, used fold
of Telegraph, the window
breathed upon and cleaned:
a fort of leatherette
and cut moquette.

All change.

The phallus of Death
thrusts in the tunnel
and lifts my hair:
amber, the flood
of light at my back,
amber and still
the backwash stone
catches my heart
in its resin and holds it—

why do I stand
so close to the edge?

Why does he stand, alone?

2

Non-indigenous green
covers the half-glazed screen
between us. You smile.
I smile.

And do we guess
veiled promises
of lunchtime grass,
of tender side-shoots
up the Public Garden path?

Passing glances
climb the glass.

The plastic pen-top
on his blotter,
blood-red in the sun,
dries its one
unflying wing.

Has life begun?

Picked up, impaled,
its shimmer fades.

Non-indigenous green
screens you
in your small cornered,
me, in mine.

3

We are all day-old:
in our broiler-house we dwell,
we will grow well and white,
well and white and stout,
we will grow upside down
with our insides clean hooked-out.

4

I want a quiet where the 5.16
does not possess each waking dream
and a train of thought, caught empty.

I want a quiet, trackless hill
where the unchained daisies fill
the growing spaces of the skull.

I want a quiet, desolate
as a folded paper plate,
as gull-cry over foam-lipped sand.

I want a quiet and a pause;
I want life's closing doors
jammed open in the climbing sun.

5

The hang of head we share
declares the death we dare not speak.
T read soft the measure of the day,
O ritual dancers of the week.

A song

As I drive my car in the morning,
my wife at my side, alone,
I wonder whether the swallows,
tumbling on the taut wires of the telephone,
speak more together of their love
or of the lovely weather?

Maybe

It is Montague and Capulet.
It is seagulls over a rookery.
It is two tall hats in the kitchen
and nobody at the sink.

Life-mask

As the years allay,
the edges embed,
the skin grows over,
the join fades.

At the back of the head
follicles split,
elastic digs in,
hair reknits.

Takes your child's,
first, unmasked fear
to wrench you back,
through thicket years,

through pain's dark maze,
to find again
your own small,
asking face

bare, wet and blind,
small fingers plucking—
plucking the tuneless
band of Death.

Mike Weatherup

Hello Mike; and how are you
   Full of yourself,
and have you measured, yet,
   full of self-doubts,
the weight of earth that holds you down,
   and worth your weight in gold.
the rate at which the chill,
   You wanted to be indispensable;
the chill already eating you,
   you damn near are—
will leave us cold? Not old, not old at all—
   and we, who sat and scoffed at you,
everyone who thought you odd,
   not knowing, Mike, the half you did,
pedantic and absurd,
   feel just as if you blew soft raspberries
feels caught-out now and rather small.
   and lunged that head and shoulders laugh
So, Michael, cheerio. Trust you
   to make us always think of you.
to disappear, so tactlessly,
   Will you be on the door
and leave us all ignoring you—
   when we come, fumbling-for-our-tickets, late?

The belly of the mind

Days when the belly of the mind
seems big with child.
It's only wind,

a painful passing flatulence
from thoughts too quickly
swallowed down

and what you proudly claim
the foetal heart,
a phantom pulse—

there's nothing there, no
chubby poem to ease into
the waiting world.

But come the day, your stomach flat
and hard from sawing wood,
from hammering nails

up on some roof, arms tight with tiles,
your waters break and then your head
is full of cries.

Envoi

Typical man,
thinks lying down for the prick of verse
is giving birth . . .

Like a warm brick

Out
into the stiff-swelling,
pink-bellied mushroom of morning
on stalks, no, on legs
of which he is hardly aware,
with a throat, which he hardly
feels, on legs weary
with walking all night,
betwixt and between
the yellow roots of dreams, which

Square
themselves to ingots
crashing only just behind him:
the door slams.

Like
a new brick,
he sucks up the morning,
like a new brick that sings,
as it sucks up the damp,
a delicate descant, before
the chorus of worries
wakens in tumult along
the bare branches; before
the dead chorus. On

Legs
lightly beneath him,
quietly farting and there,
in his chest, the unthought
thumping, I am quite happy,
as if I was dancing,
feet in perfect— and
what is that perfume?

Check

for balance,
ordering hands to pull up
pyjamas before—
as I was saying, what
is that

Per
sonal message
hands must be open
and ready for falling!

Most
intriguing.

Hands?
Must be open,
pink palms downward
over the gravel and ready

Most
gravely, and almost on tiptoe,
he's walking, triangles testing,
adjusting for balance, before
the dead chorus,
chest gently bumping,

Like
a warm brick,
carefully, humming.

Oh

Oh, I've no illusions now, said she,
Squeezing a spot from the face of the sun.
Yes, now we know where we are, said he,
Absently fiddling with the stars.
Oh yes? said a still, small voice,
Gathering the dark—

Tell you what

Tell you what, you go first.
Hide my eyes, then you hide.
Slit my fingers: peep a bit.
Well, got to cheat: only human.
Calling, come out, cooee, come out— now!
Alright, not playing anyhow.

Tell you what, count
till twenty: plenty.
Won't look, honest. Honest.
Play with myself. No: get a girl friend.
Get a girl in trouble? No. Tell you what,
get a wife: settle down, for life—

alright, till thirty then.
Alright for you! Nothing to do
but hide yourself, then,
calm as you please, tease me
from underneath the bed.
Are you calling? Not playing anyhow.

So, you sulk for years, behind
The curtain of the stars, pricking
my heart as I undo my baby's pin
and wipe her bum— now here you come,
all smiles, all open arms
and where' y' been? Not keen

and do you wonder? Well,
not counting, till it's forty, fifty,
sixty, dead? If you want any game,
God, stick around, just stick around.
Though, I'm not playing anymore; not
cheating either. Much. Tell you what—

New Town Road
for Kay and Gavin

Over the chatter of taps running,
over the head-scarved mother's scolding,
over the clack of breastbobbing
high-heels going downhill,
the toots of touch-and-go-for-the-train cars,
fuming, screeching,

over the long, slow, slithering slump of sand,
the backflap banging,
the exquisite, wincing scrape
of the clanged-down shovel
and over the rattling yawn of the sweetshop
swallowing, whole,
the gob-stopping blasphemy of schoolboys,

faintly the measure of swans' wings
planting the humped hill, calmly, behind them:
six swans, in line, going into the sun,
wings lifting, falling, solid as marble;
faint and clear, the slap of salt-water

over the smudge of a small-town morning.

To the happy couple

For Sophie and William

May you come to breakfast
and look at each other,
over the crumbs and the piles of bills,
as though you swayed on the edge of loving,
of tumbling the meeting sides of the hill.

May you find in your garden
the joys of the season
and, under a bush of merciful thorns,
exactly the wished-for measure of children:
may you never wish they were never born.

May you each be a drawerful
of tender surprises,
nothing too tangled, nothing that cuts;
at least always quick with the bandage and kisses,
forgiving and giving with no ifs or buts.

May you lie in the warm
unwrapping each wrinkle,
may you eat all love's apples yet keep some in store.
May you be better friends than lovers,
better lovers and friends than when you first swore.

Token fruit

From the apple I planted years ago
suspend two swings, one for the child
and one for the man— now doesn't that have
the beautiful ring of untruth? The poet-maggot
in the fruit becomes the sole protagonist—
jobs for the boys, his several tricky selves.
Truth is we, you and I, planted this seedling,
this great Bramley tree, thirty years gone
and three summers back I put up the swings; one
for the children of nieces and nephews and visiting
friends; the other we seldom bless with our bones,
leaving such joys to their fathers and mothers.

No, the swings and the tree are the poetry
we like to be thought as living in. We went
to some trouble— to a proper nursery
and found us a sapling too late and too big,
though a positive bargain. We heeled it in—
and too late and too big still it grows
for the child in you and the child in me.

For the child in me and the child in you
we take each Autumn our token fruit.
The rest fall heavy and bruised to the beaks
of birds and the squirrels' tooth. Such casual waste,
though nonetheless the tree accepts my hack
and slice, unfolding a dancing, canopied ark
of dazzle and dark, that should you choose
to swing below, as the petals tip their blush of snow,
what I seem to forget you then would know,
by the scent and the touch and the to and fro—
why we planted this apple tree years ago.

Lading

Each image links,
each weld decides
the tonnage held
against the ebb.

Make fast,
secure what cargo
you take past
the bar of death.

Little moth

When love touches you gently
    and tears you apart,
when your dreams are like spiders' webs
    wound round a stick,
when even the sound of his voice
    makes you sick,
then it is time to talk to your heart.
    Be still—

    Be still,
little moth in your jar. Don't you know
    this is life?
Don't you know where you are?
    Open the lid, shake
your heart free, into the air and the leaves
    of the tree.

Exhibition pots

Making sure their feet are clean,
that their best profile draws the eye,

knowing they must stand for days
just so; trying the tableau

with a stranger's glance, missing at once
the sense of touch that in the making

means so much. Disquieting. Their
frozen stares. The big ones I can more

or less ignore: they're on their own.
It is the little ones I worry for.

They cry to be picked up and filled
with necessary drink, with food,

To feel warm fingers on their skin—
I worry lest they let me down.

They go into a clumsy world of goods
that have been made to drop and bounce.

I live by brittle making and must sell.
Wave them goodbye. Wish them well.

each other
One on top of

They declare a Free-State. Mere anarchy.
They throw themselves on floors,
on chairs, on tables; take over every
inch of working surface, every door.
It gets so bad, his wife, come down
for brandy in the night, will swear
to seeing twice-worn socks enticing
virgin underwear beneath the grill. A sight

which sends her, unquenched, stumbling
to the known uncertainty of dreams.
It is not long before his shoes leave home.
His neighbours haul them back. It seems
they see them chasing cattle in the field
and fear the farmer takes a shot.
Good luck to him! – is all he says: a pause,
then, looking down – *feet, you can trust:*

they have a modicum of social sense.
Opinion is divided. The tabloids make
his life a hell. Photographers emerge
from every orifice. Sad, eager
women send him video-messages
of wardrobes full of hung, clean shirts
and numbered bags of paired-off socks
and matchless, matching underpants. It hurts

to contemplate such manic cults
but violent times up-end adults.
So, when they catch his old school tie
at Heathrow with the Ecstacy
he has himself committed, vanned away.
The sun, effulgent when they come,
shows them his room, his precious things—
the neat, squared piles of the insane.

Waste disposal

for the one without sugar

Pretty solid then? I ask, nose shut
against the stink. His is the one without.
He blows across the rim and drinks.
Eight or nine years, I reckon then,

since I last come to clear you out.
Reproved, I smile. Yes, seven or eight.
He tilts a lateral nod towards the barn.
You was doing that when I last come.

You had it all stripped down. His driver cuts
the engine and the pump. The silver armpits
of the stumped dead-elm embrace the calm.
Reflectively, he flicks an ungloved thumb.

Now that's a tree and a bit; you lost that, shame.
And for a space I see it, as it was when last he came—
grandmothering the summer air beneath
stiff skirts of dark-green bombazine: white geese,

raucous, genuflecting priests: our first grey
cats, long gone, evaporating into dappled shade.
We had it done three times. No bloody use.
Come and see the barn? Perversely

delicate they skirt the slightly hideous square
of carpet, picked up cheap to save the floor,
and tread inside heelmarks of eight or nine
years' personal waste and strain.

There's a bit of history to this place,
asserts the one without sugar. I leave his trail
to follow his gaze. All this about the Saint,
is that a con? Oh, no. Yes. All this once went

and all the land, with a Chapel that he built.
Right. He nods. There's a bit of history, then.
Better then than now, he reassures me,
offering no whys or wherefores.

We have shows here, concerts and the like.
The Arts, that's nice. He slops the dregs outside,
sidling past the carpet, handing me the mug.
Who makes these then, the driver asks? I shrug.

Me, for my sins. They look me up and down.
Yes, well – a bit of a hobby, then – that's nice.
They print their boots across the grass
and leave me to my brand-new start.

Cameo

On the morning of the village show
an old man with his walking stick,

compressed and violent as a crow,
batters fag-ends from the path

into the road. He stabs and swipes,
his free-hand welded to his knee:

a world of action shrunk to these
terse gestures of a tidy mind

still proud . . . reluctant to allow
what careless youth has left behind.

Mending windows

This is a job for half-closed eyes
and gloves. Old putty, hard as steel,
concealing these last knives of glass,
a thought too sharp and painful
to reveal. A job for reflex
and a half-closed mind.

Tempting, on still days, to do without—
but Autumn shakes its stubbled wings,
soft, beating dreams fly in at night,
rude elements will come to stay
unless this artificial screen across
affords some shelter and some light.

Given the need to use again old glass,
brittle, flawed, set in its ways, that must be
nibbled at like left-out cheese, perhaps
it might seem worth the starting fresh:
to pay the price, to draw the line—
one sweet stroke and one neat snap.

School essay
My Mum and/or my Dad

My dad is a model-maker.
His first model was dead boring.
Well it was quite clever.
It was a garden of flowering
trees and there was this man— mum
said it was just too disgusting—

all pink, in the nude,
holding his, you-know, as if he'd
just found it, it was really rude:
and this girl, blowing him kisses
and snogging this snake-thing squirming
all round her and everything, hissing.

It went to the Jumble. I liked
the next one. It was a ship.
Well, a big boat then. It took
for ever, with a roof made-up
of wood tiles, like on that Show
house, but cool, with a wood ramp

right up to the door, like the ferry
to France; and all of these animals—
my dad, he sort of gets carried away.
And, just after they laid them all off,
he took over the bathroom.
I mean, it was awful, and mum, well

mum kept not coming home.
Well, you can't blame her, this boat
floating round in the scummy
old water and all these swollen, belly-
up bodies; hundreds of people, all
looking like mum. She threw it out.

They weren't speaking for ages. Some
of the bits he must have saved
for his next thing, in the front room:
a huge, muddy, grunged-up field,
with ditches cut through, legs and arms
and dingles and dangles of old

army-bodies, hung up. Charming.
He made it by hand, the barbed-wire.
Gran went completely barmy:
made him set fire to it, said she could see
our Evie's point. Dad didn't half swear
when he picked up the poker
at the wrong end! My brother's

shoving some spuds in the embers—

The way it is

Free, with each litre of rice, a gun!
One gun, a handful of shells. All
you will ever need to be a BIG man.
All you need to kill a BIG man—
Your senior brother? The way it is.

Free, with each soldier, a ballot box!
One ballot box, a napalm bomb. Demo-
cracy? You think it saves the blackened trees
they tell you helping the world to breathe?
Don't hold your breath. The way it is.

Free, with each woman, a fatherless child,
with the special bonus get-give disease.
Tell them, grow-up: show them
your Beautiful Gun, how it gleams,
how to squeeze the trigger. The way it is.

For Hilary and John Wakeman

Call it squaring the circle,
this setting out into the sunset,
skins stretched taut over crossed Faiths.

Fifty minutes by air, oh ye Angels!
Falling to earth, dumbfound,
in an ancient Eden, unsubtled by snakes—

The woman tempted me,
but where's the harm
having the T-shirt,

the thorn-proof mittens,
the urge to grow green
in the wet living wind?

The light of Ireland

for Hilary, John, Rosie and Richie

We're early and, of course, the flight delayed.
The drive from yours was grand— a dash of rain.
We slump, be-bagged, in Bewleys Oriental Bar
to waste our little lives a little more.

People are called and called and called again.
We wander listless through to Duty Free—
more poison for more unsuspecting friends?
Being early and our flight mislaid, I scan

your book on women priests and see
the light of Ireland silver on your cheek,
the silver light of Ireland through your bones—
our little lives, our little, little lives.

Shutting my eyes, I think I see your man,
his shoulders high, his arms hung hapless down
for all as if he had been pegged outside
all night to dry in his blue dressing-gown.

People come running with their faces red.
Their flight is closed, but this is County Cork
and God being, here, so certain of Himself/
Herself is also Merciful. At last

we board and lift and bounce a bit and land
and, though we have forgotten where the car,
within the hour we step the lights of home.
Next morning we are angry, out of sorts:

I go to look for blackberries in the fog
and find them all a constipating red,
trawled thick with spider-line and dew.
Come over here, I hear that Irish laugh and know

of course, I'm only *keening on the strand*—
behind the hedge and smiling in the sun
they hang as black and fat as any where.
We sit slicing apples into the pan.

Envoi

From the well of my heart
  the water runs brown;
O, put on the kettle
  and bring on the clown!

There's bees in the gutter.
  The grass is all garlic;
O, open the bottle
and bring on the Harlots!

For Richie and Rosie
on their marriage

So, you have joined a new boat,
the Rosie Rhiannon,
tied up here hard by the Church,
soon to be sailing
into the West on the dark waters
of your man's heart.
A fair wind to you, a sweet
swell under.

Strange vessel she is, with strange
and yet to be learned
equipment and charts you may never
quite con
to your full satisfaction,
though she keep
a good bearing under your hand.
May your nets be silver with love.

No, Iain

No, Iain, there are no heroes.
Better skip after the drunken butterfly,
unfolding, unmaking the World:
sooner slide after the snake in the grass,
unstitching the intricate myths:
rather rampage through the delicate
china shop, cutting a rug,
than follow these scuff-marks over the hill,
past the bright growth where he peed in the grass,
the slight pit where he spat in the dust—
Iain, there are no heroes, although
you may stumble a similar path,
making excuses as you go.

Knot-songs

I

So often right
for the wrong reasons,

man, woman:
impossible vows.

Later, legs locked together,
hearts beating on opposite sides,

ill-managed attempts on bliss,
down the dark labyrinth of eyes.

Silently sitting at breakfast, feeding
The sly silk of fear through the ring

on the finger: for better, for worse—
So often wrong for the right reasons.

I

You lie against me
and you weep
and I love you—
will you sleep?
Will you sleep;
wet, on my chest,
your cheek. You turn.
What other harbour
would you seek?

III

Damp evening. Late.
Sour wind, off made-up land.
The worst is over. Half-asleep,
he takes a turn around the park
and only two half-hitches stand
between him and the hungry dark.

IV

For reasons of its own
Love takes the long way round;
may, on occasion, not appear at all.

Smashed in some ditch?
A double-puncture in a country lane?
Some other nonsense simply not explained?

We wait. The food grows cold.
The music stops. We drink too much
and fall asleep— Love is here: our bleary rage

rolls over on its back
and beats its tail. Or else— someone
official comes and answers us that Love is dead.

Lust, meantime,
steals the cakes before they cool,
makes fools of clever girls and catches

sage old men
as tight as curls in guilty zips.
Lust jumps the fence. Lust breaks the gate.

Lust blows the locks,
and, laughing, burns this black-edged hole,
through which to gaze on hate.

Sorry

There's saying sorry
  and there's saying sorry.

I say, *I'm sorry*.
  That's not sorry.

No more with cold

Today I gathered flowers you grew
and put them in a vase, still hot,
to set them on my stall of pots
glowing in the Autumn rain

and as the rain ran down my neck
and as my scalp and hands grew cold
I thought how you and I grow old—
and then it came,

the smile that I could think like this
and see your flowers and my good making
and know that I was here and shaking
no more with cold than happiness.

New Year '98

Winds blow, tides turn, moons wax and wane,
the dead year flips its coin again—
heads we are rich, tails we are poor
so call the coin and wish for more.

Despite the frosts new buds will chance,
despite the years old feet will dance—
tails we are poor, heads we are rich
and either way we think too much

who walk beside the circling sea
and sing the wave and taste the spray,
being in this both rich and poor—
the sea-wrack on each other's shore.

For Dad

In early March, as buds were breaking,
I stroked your hair and watched you dying.
Your feet were cold. I fetched a bottle.
Bye now, I said and walked away.

High summer now. Rain on the velux:
jaunty dance of fife and drum. I feel
your cold feet, Dad, step briskly
through the wet flowers in my head.

Should I call after you, so quick
to make you turn and fetch your death?
No. I hated so the slowing down that killed you—
I'll come behind you, out of breath.

Indoor fireworks

The hardest lessons are the little ones.
We squat together by the fire:
mother, father, child. Our daughter
kneels and sings as, failing one by one,
these non-explosive, sad, brown
travesties enrage my bad boy's heart.
It yearns the secret fireworks we made,
each tailored for a bigger bang,
as dustbin-lids came clanging down
through poisonous palls of pale-puce smoke.
No one we knew got hurt,
so where's the harm?
So where's the good?
She rocks and sings, our little one.
For her it is enough; the firelight,
the breath held back against the cough,
the charred, salt-petre smell,
the slow, slow burning edge of love.

Morning Magics

The silk-fog lifted.
The whole audience stood frosted.
Then, he smiled.

Trees dropped their buds of glass.
Turned-earth pinkened.
Grass blushed green.

Seeing is believing

Morning. Hard and white.
The barn roofs lead themselves with frost
and in the green, sun-slanted grass lies red
the belly of a rat,
ill-met with death in my grey cat.

Late afternoon. Toasted and green
the barn roofs rub against the sun
and, in the purple-shadowed grass,
charred, black-edged, red,
a wrapper from our thin-sliced bread.

Ill-served by memory, the gut
brings-up again what never was—
I grimace, dangling unseen fur.
The dustbin clangs.
Between my legs a grey cat purrs.

So

So, the crouched hare was a turned stone,
  the running fox, a rag on thorns,
  the poised hawk, a clapping dove—

and love, quick, trembling love,
  a lucky, collared water-drop
  from a leafy, ducked-through door?

Barn floor
for Sophie

When he did this, he was not doing this.
With elegant irrelevance
he danced this foot-maze in the floor.

When I saw this, I saw no more
than cat pursuing moth across
fresh concrete's shrinking water-skin.

When he did this, I stood and swore,
the cleaned-off float clutched in my fist—
but, bending now to brush the dust

cradled in each timeless print,
when I do this, I see his dance,
his magic murder of the moth.

When I see this, I see your cat,
eyes-open-blaring at my curse,
and laugh at it, but can't forget,
now he is dead, I wished him worse.

The cat has a mouse

Age brings something—
don't tell me Wisdom!
I'd settle for Cowardice,
though who's to judge
my natural drawing-back as such?

The cat has a mouse under the chair.

Age must bring something—
shall we say, lying-awakeful
with no expected trial tomorrow,
no test to take? As well,
considering the memory cell.

The cat has a stalemouse under this chair.

Age will bring something—
a parcel wrapped in best
bombazine black. I shall put it
away, under the stairs,
for a rainy-day, some rainy day.

The mouse has the cat under her spell.

Age—bring yourself! Sit here
in the sun this spring-loaded morning.
Laugh your dry spit at that damn
monotonous blackbird
with only one tune in his neck.

The cat's forgotten just what the game is.

Age, you and I will wallow and natter
and doze and dream snapshots in letters
from neat-nippled girls,
all smiles in the sun—
we are their elders and betters.

We have a cat and a mouse and two chairs—

The secret of the now

Two kittens and a cardboard box
explain the secret of the now—
life as pretend:

the wolf outside,
the wolf within.
Let the game of life begin.

I shrink inside my thin pink skin
and watch the clock
stand still above such savagery

and wonder how imagining,
for humans, has become
so much of fear and waiting death,

so little left of breathless joy
that puts its claws into the dark
and finds its little brother there.

The dividend

This lovely, silenced hour of dark,
this unlooked, unearned dividend,
when you can sit and think and not be doing,
when you can let the thoughts that don't bear thinking
claw up your legs into your lap,
when you can stroke their ears and set them purring,
when you are still alive and gently breathing,
your fingers in the subtle fur of death.

Symbolically speaking

Where does the heart go when the heart
goes out of you?

Not talking viscera here, not talking
cell counts or ventricles,

more your actual, symbolic heart, your nub,
your centre, the where

you are nailed in time and space. Where
does it go when it's had it

completely? Does it go dancing?
A final fling? Some

sense of rythym must have rubbed off.
Does it make the effort,

or is it so down it slumps in a corner
at some shady table

joining the slop-rings, matching the lipsticks
left on the stubs,

pretending the touch of fingernails, light,
but sharp, on the back of the hand?

Are there shoes that come clacking, are there
lips that part, symbolically

speaking, that part to reveal the teeth,
the symbolic smile,

curling the toes under the table, the smile
that asks for a light,

that tells the sad heart a sadder story
ending in laughter—

and what, symbolically speaking,
comes after?

His best work

He does his best work in the half-light
of morning.

This is when his sadness is most clear,
least muddied

by tidal sediments of joy stirred up
each given day.

In the backwash of dawn, his maiden soul,
languishing

gracefully in the fetid prison of his body,
transparently

aches to slip free with the first notes
of birdsong

onto the winds of a bright March morning,
lies weeping

finding herself bound in the stiff muscle,
the rough,

untouchable skin of this alien
earthbound thing—

yet this is when he does his best work,
delicate,

longhand, before he falls back,
snoring.

The grind of shingle

The grind of shingle under the keel
in that hanging moment as you leap
to meet the cold, the wet, the real—

this is the dream our shallows reveal
in the homecoming lurch of final sleep,
to grind of shingle under the keel.

No, sleep it is not: this isn't the deal—
the soul seeks its landfall, no drop too steep,
to meet the cold, the wet, the real,

for the senses are gone with which to feel
if the footing be warm or cold or deep.
The grind of shingle under the keel

no more than the delicate peal
of rain on dusty Summer glass. Weep
not for cold, for wet, for real –

tomorrow your urgent soul
may be leaning a new life, into the slap,
from the grind of shingle under the keel,
into the cold, the wet, the real.

Disengendered

a bedtime story

And, when I learned I must not be a man,
because I cared and had the gift to kill,
I left my father's house and stowed away:
but not the first, no, not that rusty ship
with fenders hung like crosses down its side:
the Holy Tub, already sitting low. No,

I slipped a little farther on, pulled
by the laughter and the shapely tilt
into the greasy basin. Oh, it was easy,
no watch being kept,
I crept inside a yielding coil of rope.
My land was gone: daylight when I woke.

And what are you? The fierce women said.
I'm just a boy. A special boy, they laughed.
Then they began to talk the Mother-tongue,
odd words of which I had, but not the sense
except that, for the moment, I was safe,
provided that I mind my Ps and Qs.

And so I sailed away into my days
and lay awake at night, under the stars,
numb with the ache to kill and not to care.

They taught me *Walking Round The Witch*,
the kinder ones with signs and gentle shoves—
though there were those whose greatest love
seemed to instruct exactly, with neat words,
then, standing back to watch you stumble wrong,
to catch you fast against their smothering legs

Till you fell dead. Then they all breathed
you back again. Learn this, they said,
and you'll be useful to us soon. The trick
was in the study of their hands. Their eyes
unreadable and full of smiles, their bodies,
oh, their soft beguiling breasts and thighs—

but, as you step towards them, you must watch
their hands for any slightest stir or twitch,
for what they touch those hands will always hold.
At last they dropped me in some foreign port.
I walked the quayside in the falling dark.
The rusty ship rode higher now, its crosses

slumping loose, like broken men.
I followed the rank scent of beer
into a room of shoulders and of sweat
which let me through, not seeing I suppose
the inbetween I had become. A woman there,
when I refused her pretty overtures,

threw back her throat and pointed with her chin
and screamed, he's one of those! Piss-off,
you useless Mother-fucker you!
and, thus it was, I came at last to kill.
They did not know you had to watch the hands.
I left the bar-room full of gasping dead—

Then, taking ship, I look for better lands.
I squat for years in this quiet cave,
where thought distils like water from the walls.
Then comes this present crop of wars
and dreams drag by my cave-mouth, refugeed.
I take them in and give them bed and food

till now I am the mother of a tribe,
till now I am the father of grown sons
who sing of how they kill without a care.

For Sophie

now eleven

Though when I saw that one and one make three,

yes, saw you shaken from the dark and loving sleeve,
a pink and purple mitten on a thick and pumping string,

though then, poor fool, I took you for a boy,

I didn't mind the midwife scoffed me right.
Relief, perhaps? Red-faced, I would not need
to stand and watch you kick some grubby ball
past my old jumper into goal, or teach you,
God-forbid, to throw a punch. Once, as a boy,
is really quite enough. Outnumbered though

by one and one entrancing into three—

your mother comes and takes me by the hand.
We listen, laughing, by your bedroom door.

I don't, it's you, Daddy, who snores.

Ah, yes, you make me wrong, you put me right,
so right that nothing can be wrong—
my dear untidy daughter, you who hold,
within your perfect inner rooms,
a million goals kicked at and missed,
a million punches never to be thrown.

Fifteen

for a certain photograph of Bundle

Strangers and friends alike stand gazing at
blushed cheeks, browned eyes and blonded wisps
and sometimes, taken in, give out that
nowadays such art is rare, reason eclipsed
by our child's semblance to this
child of two.
Child of two,
like each of us, stirred bright-hot
in the four-legged melting-pot;
strange alchemy of bodies, mingling to a shout
of echoes and forebodings none can single out—
for who can accurately map or trace
whose look passed then across your face
when you were little more than two
and, in a stanger's studio, sepia recorded you?

A faker's farewell
to the good old days

Today, he does not write. Today
he closed a good old door, for good:
a stable-door. Well, yes, long after
the mushroom breath of the horse,
long after the ziss of milk in the pail.
A hundred and fifty years farewell:
screwed-down and sealed with silicone
and foil-backed foam. Out side
it looks the same; big-hinged
and patched and tarred, the latch
cross-hatched to keep the witches out,
his daughter's Holy-holey stone
still hanging on frayed baler-twine.

In side, he nails a poem from
the bottom up. He beats the planks
to give them age. He creosotes a history
and washes it with plaster-white
and furnishes with burnished iron;
this fine old fake that will not serve
for anything but looking at.
A door to keep the wild world out,
to make you smile. More real or less?
Let's say, less mealy-mouthed than verse.

Chinese poem
for Inga

At the house of a hundred teapots
there was wine and laughter
and sweet foods: and you, careful
lest we should not be content,
anxious should cruel words settle
like flies on the sweetmeats— but,
laughter and wine
and no flies.

I have gone South.
In my garden, the aquilegia
thrust green fists of dew
through nodding snowdrops.
When chestnut-buds break,
I shall come North.
Perchance, we shall meet
in the chattering Market.
We shall talk teapots
and wine and laughter.

We shall keep the World waiting,
while Winter gives the cold shoulder to Spring.

For Bob Burlingham

I woke with you between my ears:
sound, sight and touch. The smell
of cigarette in your good clothes,
the smile Sinatra would have killed for,
zipping your Bogart-upped-a-class.

Musician, painter, angel of dry wit,
I still curl-up at your sly cuttings-down
to size: you purger of pi-hypocrites,
who, quite despite yourself and me,
found fondness, cuckooing contempt,
for my light talent and flush youth.

We watch you boxed and rolled away,
through discretion's muffled doors
and, while you queue for earthly fire,
the family faces lose the rigor of your death:
relaxing into how, so-typically, you let
them down by dying with their promises
so wilfully left unachieved. Anger,
pretending grief, at best relief: although
your widow, young enough to be your child,
lifts up her head and weeps to Mozart,
making his bargain with the dead.
I say some words: a joke for you—
the family face averted from my lack of taste.

You knew the rules.
You knew you had to die—
that this was one small contretemps
you could not chassis wryly round—

ah, dear smiler with the knife,
I wish you a charmed afterlife.

For Liz

Now you are less, Liz,
than someone's white, wet handkerchief
that rolls between the cleaned, parked cars:

now you are spilling
from the careful, seaward wind, caustic
among the labelled reek of loving wreaths:

oh, how I wished
you'd show a leg through the blue, swish
velvet curtains, through the valley of the shadow,

through the shocked,
pink-rimming mourners. Dear departed,
now you are smoking your last, one-too-many,

just for me,
say something damnable, hilarious,
or lift a wry plucked eyebrow, flick

that tall stack
with your finger, brush the ash from your black
skirt and cough maliciously and laugh.

Open verdict

for Edgar

In the Great Hall, at Christmas, you caught me
thundering up and down the twin-staircase,
fingers poked tight in both ears, trying to learn,
through my feet, how it feels to be deaf like
the boys you unlocked the mouthing-world for.
How quiet you stood, one hand caressing
a branch of the giant Christmas tree, bending
it down. How quiet, as you looked up, turning
my stomach to stone, to gurgling water.
Then how you laughed, dismissing the grim
headmaster, becoming again my favourite uncle
calling the dog and me to heel. A natural Lord
you seemed to me then, trotting beside you,
in awe of the gun held sure but careful, staring
in town-boy wonder at the hare's form
you stepped over, lifting me gently aside:
shocked and delighted when, at my whim,
you stopped and took aim, clipping
that pine-tree top with your first barrel—
a dead shot.

I treasure the scar of your soft,
fierce laughter, the rookery's black confetti
of swearing.

Recalling, there on your workshop
wall, in elegant, challenging black and white,
THERE IS NO SUCH WORD AS CAN'T,
it's hard to conceive the implacable frown,
haunting each family photograph,
giving way to any weakness but rage
or savage laughter. Now, nearing your age,
with pride I remember your lean arms around me,
me steering your Standard Ten car, at ten
miles an hour.

Here, deep in this cluttered drawer,
the tape we made of the 78 of you leading prayers

one Deaf School morning: your voice, my voice.
Though, were they here, those upturned faces
would not confuse for they could not compare.

For us also, such a fall of silence like sudden snow.
Aged fourteen, I enter the little front parlour,
my mother's breath going out on your name
like a smothered candle, *oh, Edgar, Edgar . . .*

A blanket of shame, long trodden and melted,
summers and winters and now, spring-cleaning,
I stumble across these pine shelves I stripped
of your oak-stain and beading, making them fit
for a newer fashion: your frown, now
as then, shutting the hole in my head too late
on the icon of you, sagged over a woodland gate,
twitching and bleeding; wide over the grounds
of the lordly house the rooks circling, screaming.

O, wonderful uncle, dying so little known,
did you burn so bright you just burned down?
Did love run out like a cooling bath?
Surely your feeling for wood must have
told you the rail of the gate was rotten?
You climbed it most out-of-term days.

Deep in the thorns of the daily thicket,
such simple things are simply forgotten?

I have only the gossip of rooks to go by;
the desperate, hesitant trot of the dog
coming home, at last, alone.

Living alone
for Auntie Roddy

Living alone,
her paintings lean
like fresh-faced children
by each chair,
against each wall.
She tugs them out
to tell their faults,
half-praising some,
but loving all.

Funny old stick,
not much to look at—

her words, not mine, but true:
though she is not the simple sum
of all life gave and took away.

To her, like yesterday, the time
her father wept for her lost hair—

bobbed short to catch the boys
she let come through
the library-gate into her heart;
who changed their books
and smiled and left her prisoner there.
Her uncorrected eyes
looked both ways then,
seeing their point of view
and, through the tears, her own.

Was it too much to ask?
Wanting it all to be hers,
hating to have to let go,
needing to have and to hold?

You'll have it when I'm gone, dear—

Absurd. Absurd, but not,
that I remember, ever
a spiteful word. Bossy, gentle,
firm with her garden, her dreams—

talking in one busy breath of Paris,
of fresh potted-meat,
of so many things—

seeing the world both ways,
embracing, to the last ache,
all life left her—
            living alone.

Song

In the Garden in my head
sit all my people who are dead,
in the sunshine, at their ease—
gone the doubt and gone the pain.
As they wait to pour the teas
the worst they fear is summer rain—

and the words I left unsaid,
words of love, the words of hate,
shine in the grass about their feet,
daisy, speedwell, buttercup—

    and I am known. They hear
    my thought. They all look up . . .

Valediction

For Dad

Against the plumped white of the pillow
your face is yellow as the clay.
I stroke your hair. You frown. You open eyes

as slate and far away as that salt sea
that Mum was so enamoured of. *Who's that?*
He sounds like Mum— it could be her.

Strange how Northamptonshire the voice,
the BBC discarded like a carapace
and suddenly I see the both of you, before

your grey-haired boys were born, her arms
tight round you on the motorbike, squealing
not to go too fast, hoping in her heart you would.

The past forgets sometimes to be the past.
My future is in you, you said.
You could not quite believe a life to come—

though God's accounts looked elegant
you could not make them total true,
or sign your name in that neat fist—

though in the audit of the inner ear,
could you have only carried one,
might it have been a different sum?

So there you are, still clinging on,
though this opponent is too big, too tough
for mortal man. You've kept your guard up

all your days and ridden all that life could throw
and we all know your famous left-hand jab,
so rude it floored the best of us— but what

the referee, what all the judges could not see,
those sly, unlooked-for kindly acts
that should have let you win on points.

Ah, well, the fight was fixed and I confess
I'm glad the final bell has gone and, yes,
the coin of childish love for you

I pocketed long years ago has worn
a silent hole and slipped clean through
and, at my feet, shines new again.

You ask what time it is. You close your eyes
against the dark. *God bless*, you say
deliberate and clear, *God bless—*

and you too, Dad. And you too, Dad.

Should we?

Should we speak ill of the dead?
Perhaps it is what they need
to bring them alive again.

Perhaps a few home truths,
a few well chosen curses
would seem to them more use

than everything cut short
in silence and excuses.

These winters between

Midnight— 31st December 2000

Do I wait— have I been waiting, these winters between,
to forget, to forgive, to be forgiven? Mother? Mum—
your sideways face as grey as the skated ice
that cracked the song from your skull, as white
as the grass turned magical snow. Blind with snow.

I am three. I know this is serious. I am taking your hand
in the two of mine. I put out my strength. My feet go from me.
I am down on my knees. I am hauled away. Someone takes me.
There are people all round you. Being no use, I am borne away.

So life betrays us. Puts us firmly out of our place.

Moments before you were laughing, skating so gaily, lost
in the wildness of joy. I saw— I think I remember seeing
the fingers of grass grope out of the ice, catching
the nose of your skate as you came by. You didn't die.
You lived, with your headaches, that dragged you on all fours
upstairs to your bedroom of tight-drawn curtains,
big-eyed and white. Quiet, muffled days. That little boy
enveloping that seed of ice, has felt it grow, has sensed
the darkness of the outer shell— now prising from
its mother-of-pearl this soft and precious memory,
rolls it in his big, creased palm, pops it warm into his mouth,
savours the taste, sucks it, winter on winter back to the grit—

so life rewards us when we least— yes, when we least.

For Gavin

milking.
swing and thump, sweet, singing hiss:
leaning into her gargling side,
into the ache of this sawn thumb,
and this torn teat
and if
the afterlife is void of this
unclean, lush, permeating smell,
this comfortable, niggling pain,
squealing, you're here, you're here,
you are
you are, you are—
she's done,
I wipe her off and lead her back
across the yard and, turning, skip
her steaming stepping stones— no,
if
the afterlife has none of this
then, wipe me off,
lead me back
into the pungent
dark.

For Caromy and Simon Shannon
12th September 1999

She lifts her face as everyone watches
in the Church crammed tight as a box of matches.
She is making herself an icon, this girl,
this girl in white, lifting her chin
with a smile that none of us will forget:
a cup of delight filled to the brim,
bubbling over, drowning him—

> He is lost, he is done for: look at his face.
> Not a man in these pews wouldn't take his place.

Outside, on the sloping green of the hill,
she is loud as a fourth-year let out of school.
She is making us all an example, this girl,
as the chains of marriage whirl in the sun
like unbelievable freedoms won,
as she shares what she has, as she gives,
as she takes outrageous liberty for all our sakes—

> He is lost, he is done for: look at his face.
> Not a man in this churchyard would not take his place.

Moonfable

For Dora

I lie in my bed
and stare at the moon.

Politely she asks,
If you grow up what will you be?

Rudely, I chant *the dish ran away*
with the spoon.

The Moon steps close.
She puts out her tongue. She licks my face.

Take my place?
Oh sure, I sneer, *if pigs could fly*. *Well, the cow*

jumps over the Moon,
she murmurs, suddenly fast at my side—

Before I can think,
before I can blink, I am up in the sky.

She lies in my bed,
her face so white. They kiss her.

They shake her.
She will not wake. Pale in the sky,

in the hot afternoon,
I fade in the sun like a let-go balloon.

Song

for Sophie

You sun-brown sprawler, socks-off in the hay,
things grow themselves

I see you sing and stroke and daisy-chain
things die themselves

your little gold-eyed special cat— the one
do all you can

you trod in bleak turned earth today
do nothing bad

and in the van, with cat-peed trousers off
things go away

you cry— **she must come home, come home—**
try as you might

you line with patted hay the brutal hole,
keep them close

you lend your weight to her light soul . . .
hold them tight

For my daughter

That trick I taught you yesterday
of Giants falling from the sky—
you draw him right way up
then turn the page to add
the beanstalk and young Jack
calmly leaning on his axe—
that trick may serve you well, my girl,
when you are grown and I am old.
Those words I hedge about your world
making a maze where non-sense rules
so you may play, so you may fret
part princess and part prisoner,
forgive.
Forgive
also my laugh, seeing you frown
trying to logic my tall walls down.
Those words will puzzle only me
when you are grown and stepping free.

> Daddy, in your drawer today
> I found this poem, done for me,
> and, though it made me furious,
> I hear you smiling, catch your laugh
> and know the lines were kindly meant.
> Well then, dear Giant, fallen from the sky
> who let me steal the Golden Hen
> and pluck the music next your heart,
> who dreamed with one eye open all the time,
> who tried to give me a fair start
> and told me to be careful with my facts,
> it was not me who used the axe—
> though, were it now to hand, I'd lay
> Time's hedge to keep you high enough
> to let you see your daughter's lands.

What touching?

What breaks my dream and wakes me, stops me lifting
the Driftway gate across the black quag's silken steaming;
what tender ache this late-warm, winter morning?

This sideways slap of sun? The slow, deliberate, undoing
gape of calloused skin? The blood-red buds sharp pricking—
that single, celebrating clap of ring-doves wings?

Or is it this? This under-everything embrace hefting
the five-barred mind across the mire; the drifting
hum within the wind, that leaves me light and singing?

Soundbite

Ah, yes— this is the meat of the matter.
We've finally reached it. What, may I ask,

did you think you were doing?
What, after all, were you here for?

In a few words, please— we're
running out of time. Thank you.

I'm afraid we must end there.
I'm sorry to have to cut you off—

Tomorrow we'll be looking at Time.
Will it ever, in fact, run out?

Valentine

No stem-rose.
No satin-heart.
No sugared rhyme.
No one to guess at.
No bliss of hurt.

Only a filthy boiler-suit
to empty out the pockets of, dust
on your working-surfaces—
wrong colour mud
and on the white rim
of the bath, gorgeous as innards
of a shell, the shucked-off plaster,
sepia and blush from my blood-blister—

for I am hammering
your Valentine,
with four-inch nails,
through wood that once was red with wine,
through wood that once was red with wine.

Make sure

In the back-alley of my head
I kick a ball against the wall
and think of how I won't grow up,
never, not ever at all—
though I might go away a bit
on holidays and there I'll fly
my Spitfire through the burning sky
and ride my pony up the gulch
to where my laughing killers wait—
whichever way I come to die
make sure you chew your plaits
and cry . . .

What are we to do with them all?

What are we to do with them all,
these tribes locked in their little valleys
by the difficult mountains of history?
What else can we do but give them the means
to defend to the death the things they believe in
as we would ourselves. Yes, we are lucky,
set in our silver sea, our silver lining—
though, you make your own luck, don't you think?

What are we to do with them all?
Surely we must, when the devil drives,
supply whatever *machinery* they need.
Not to supply lets others in on the act:
we don't do it— others will. Just think
of the factories gone, our balance of payments.
The proof of the pudding— the Dow is up,
the Footsie rising. In this life you need
a competitive edge. You can't make
an omelette without breaking—
not our eggs of course, though we're
not counting chickens. What we must do is
to show the State-of-the-Art such tribes
can aspire to, if they ever get out of the mire
that evil bastard is treading them into.

What are we to do with them all,
nightly trudging their pain through our monitors,
over the broken ground of our hearts? The rag-doll
women, thrown down, trampled, pushed back
to their children, to the stunned old men. Enough!
Enough to make a strong man weep, to wet himself—
But are we to blame? We are doing our best.
Tell me, is it for us to send our mother's sons?

What are we to do with them all?
Too easy to misunderstand our intent:

too easy to stand on a shaking bridge and offer
brave fists to the oncoming sky if you're high
on hate, on lies, on scandalous propaganda.

What are we to do with them all? All
suggestions welcome. No? So be it.
We keep on sending wave after wave
till they come to their senses. It has to be
done. Does anyone want a Third World War?

Yes, yes of course I'll covenant my donation.
That way we all do our bit for the poor.
Though I've said it before, I'll say it again,
what are we to do with them all?

What are we to do with them all?

Throwaway knife

The edge I came with
scares me stiff.
I keep it hidden,
safely sheathed.

Sometimes I turn
its wicked point
in on myself—
to no effect,

these little pockmarks
all I've made
given the plastic
shielded blade.

Sometimes I sit and run
the handle, bright
as blood, between
my fingers in the sun.

A day for

A day for pegging out of dreams,
for propping up the sagging line
between the Maytree and the Oak:
how sweet the smell of coming clean.

Despite the sly particulates
free-loading on the Autumn wind,
doubts dwindle in the sliding sun:
we kick like kids through crisping leaves,

hearts lifting as the letters drop.
Like kids our faces fall— one letter
from a love-locked friend, two overdues
and half-an-acre of tall trees traduced

to make us offers which we bin—
this Future we are driving to, this sense
of flesh and bone suborned, reduced
to glossy dreams. Somewhere, intent, obscene,

God, clicking at a cosmic screen,
downloads your innermost desires
to pander them to some dot.com?
Tomorrow comes, will not be brushed aside.

No matter with what dash you drive
you cannot keep ahead of time.
No matter that you chanced today,
bronze-shoudering your clumsy car,

a rough-legged buzzard, lilting on the wind—
though, let it be a Talisman.
O, hard head with the golden eye
look out for me— spread wide

your feathered fingertips against the time
I wet myself, against the time
I ring the bell, the time the money's gone
and no one comes . . .

Bananas

Hot white family. Red, red road. A trestle
of small green bananas. Nigeria then.

Parking the car forty years later,
across a grey road, my birthday daughter

Soon it will afternoon-rain.
We flap the doors of the Austin and eat.

stands in her doorway, exotic, chaotic
like something out of the nose-studded jungle—

We wave at the picaninny. Good bananas!
Waxy. Sweet. Five for the penny. Her white teeth.

Clutching our gifts, the cake, some spotty bananas,
we wait for the cars as she blows us kisses.

We wave and away as the red road spots the black car
with warm drops of blood. The wipers complain.

It is starting to rain. Like tourists we stand
at the edge of her future, unsure of ourselves.

The family waving to a big white smile,
Mum saying, 'Poppet: you felt you knew her—'

Our child, how well we know her? Hardly at all—
I start to cross— I drop the bananas. I curse. I smile.

If all the cracks

If all the cracks in the pavement
were lined-up, end-to-end,
they'd stretch from here to Kingdom come
and all the fears and all the tears
and all the things you mustn't do
would run to where they all belong
and split the Universe in two.

Inside the old man a boy holds a frog in both hands,
inside the old woman a girl still chews her bright hair.

If all the cracks in the pavement
were laid-down, side-to-side,
you'd see that there was nothing there
but rained-on earth the sun has dried
and all the things you never saw
and all the things you never tried
stood open like a Summer door.

Inside the old woman the girl still skips and sings,
inside the old man the boy is bouncing, bouncing the ball.

A wave less certain

Coming over the ridge
I slow on seeing the man
in a lime coloured jacket peeing
invisibly into the hedge. Shaking
himself, the bike propping
his back topples. Cursing
he rights it and, wheeling
it on, his face burnt brick,
gives me a lordly wave of the hand
and another, less certain, of his prick.

Forsythia

The sad Forsythia you cut in twig
two weeks ago, is blithe in bloom:
more butter in its yellow than these daffs,
that shake and tremble in the fluted glass,

that sense the snow-grains in a wind
leaned-in from the Arctic shore, a wind
that slices through the newly clinkered
cellar-floor. You sigh. You lift your feet

into the warm and snuggle down into your
read, one hand caressing, crabwise, to the cat.
Outside, snow devils dance and twitch and spin:
the bones ache with the hate of it.

I think of how you flower in the sun.
I think of how you clutch the raft of home.
The wind slots in another Stanley blade.
I walk the daffs into a kinder room.

Poet

Jackdaw. Hit and miss. Feeding twigs
down a gaping chimney pot, like a mother
feeding hope, hoping something sticks
in life's black throat, to press a shape of feathers in.

Oh yes. The fire's long dead. Look. Look at all
my shiny bits and bobs, bright odds and ends
of images; a treasury of stolen truths.
Beak full, I fall into the fireplace. I shake.
I stretch my wings and smack into the glass.

What's this? Strange thumb-marks on the clouded pane,
there and there and there again. From smudged centres
radiate imperfect whorls, there and there— and here
the culprit caught, translucent sepia in the silver sun
gathering water over and over, waving arms in
strict spider order, scraping in the stuff of life,

making signs for me to read as fingered glass.

I sit and chew my pen. Twigs fall. The fireplace fills
with balls of soot. Paint peels from the window cill.
The sun stands up and slowly steps away.

Calmly, I condense my thoughts.

A silver strand

For Bundle

A silver strand from the crown of your head,
caught like a snake in this spider's web,
flicks in the wind to the kiss of the sun—

a dead thing living is Death undone.

Small-brown butterfly, fret-worked wings
closed stiff in my fist, though the dry feet cling;
so, bear him out to the breezy green—

a dead thing living is Death unseen.

My stomach melts to the bend of your back,
you, pulling up plants, your fingernails black
as you barrow the makings of next year's earth—

a dead thing living is Death reversed.

Villanelle

My pocket is empty of all but fluff.
Shall I turn it out in the Autumn wind?
Once it was full of all sorts of stuff—

a half-chewed apple, my mother's love,
those smirking Angels— all since binned.
Now my pocket's empty of all but fluff,

though fluff is not nothing, indeed enough
to engage the fingers and puzzle a mind
once full of all sorts of stuff, such stuff,

all manner of thoughts, both fine and rough,
thoughts to loose and thoughts to bind—
now my pocket's empty of all but fluff.

Little better, you'd think, than a lost glove
stuck on the fence for the loser to find.
Once it was full of all sorts of stuff,

dreams and ambitions, desires that drove
me out of my depth and staring blind—
yes, I was full of such sorts of stuff.
Now, my pocket is empty of all but fluff.

Because of predicted frost

Already our breath shows on the dark air.
We hat the paeonies and young delphiniums
with sheets of your ma's old Telegraph,
for once forgoing last week's excitements
on account of the cold and the present need.
We judder indoors leaving a flock of moonbirds,
bent-winged and feeding, guarding the tender
just budding spikes under the halogen stare of light.

Last cup of tea. Watch the News. Out of green jungle,
bandaged and dying, the tribe come carrying
shrivelled children, huge-eyed under the scanning
for guns, for items of value. Still, soon they are home,
back to the places of blood and bone, the honed edges
of rusty questions. A mother with new, presumed innocent
baby, photogenically glad to be back in Rwanda, ogles
the lens, looking quite well. Switch off. Camomile. Bed.

In the morning, it's enough to make you weep—
green carnage. So many stricken but bravely
standing, necks broken, leaves limp: those
that have kept their white flags just in with a chance.
A Red-Cross, helicoptering sun swings slowly by
attempting a reckoning. You scrumple the news.
You sigh. You shrug. Too far North, you say. It's fine.
I mean, they're only plants— they're only plants.

Recycled
Cambridge style

Up goes the lid of the bin: me,
doing my slightly furtive thing—taking out
what most, for the general good, put in—
find, under a picture of poor Rabin

GUNNED DOWN BY A JEW, a breath
straight from the unwashed vat of death.
Blond wisps on wine-bruised skin,
the side of the top of a head,

a tweed-jacketed shoulder. I lower the lid.
Not shocking. Not shocked. Quite matter-of-fact,
a sign of the times. Take colours to read,
broadsheets for wrapping, back to the stall.

Tell it to no one— protected, the dormouse.

Come back to check and you never were.
No blond curls, no well-worn tweed.
Just a concave heave, a hint of swirl
where something gaped and gulped you down.

Fresh deposits of three year's notes:
pink parcel corseleted in string—
even the odour of wine has gone,
even the odour of wine and skin.

60p

It opens with the door, the smell
of worn, remembering things. I take it in:

the till, the baskets, the third-world
bric-a-brac, egg-slice, toast-rack,

lampshade, whisk. Five cups on an Oxfam shelf
and one of them is— four are white,

transferred with flowers, remnants of sets
each with its unknown factory mark,

thin, moulded china handles swinging neat
on curl-eared cuphooks— but the handle

of the fifth's too wide and not the proper shape.
Handmade, unstamped, pot-bellied, squat,

a salt-glazed ugly-duckling of a pot,
wheel-thrown, edge chipped and stained,

at 60p ten pence more than any of the other four
and just about the asking price when,

six or seven years ago, hot to the touch,
I took it shining from my kiln

and rubbed its bristled bottom smooth
and sent it out into the world.

Amazed, I shake my head and hang
my baby back. Somewhere a window

with a yoghurt pot of basil or of marjoram
awaits this damaged brat of mine. I pay the ladies

at the till for someone else's trousers
I have never met but seriously intend to wear.

Talisman

I make a special trip into the dark
to pick it up.
I can't pretend— I have pretended
all day long
I didn't see just what it was,
straight off.

I walk the four-brick path towards
the pottery.
The light comes on and there it is,
a brown faced flint,
with dirt for eyes and nose and mouth—
my kiss of death.

I stoop to pick it up. I take it cold
to my hot hand,
back through the smiles of battered flowers
now shrugging off
two days of brutal wind. A gentler night.
Indoors I rinse

the skull to find a face with one good eye
that fixes me, try as I might to stare it out. I take
my talisman
to bed. I lay me down. I make an eyes-wide trip
into the dark.

Hiccup

The kiln is behaving, no more silly buggers,
no burnt out connections, no elements gone.
Already it's clonking off and on like a hiccuping
barrel— the workshop hot as a dragon's bowel.
An hour to wait while the kiln soaks. Hiccup. Hiccup.
I swipe my face on a clay-stiffened towel. An hour,
then sleep— then back to the slip-in-slip-out-of
bandage of bed. I tidy the boards of unfired pots.
I tell them soon it will be their turn, soon I shall
pack them shoulder to shoulder, shelf on shelf,
lower the lid and burn them out of their brittle
into immutable ill or good— this hiatus a hiccup.

Life playing at being a zip that sticks, neither up
nor down, neither this nor that, the hanging
half-open fuddled mind all fingers and thumbs—
no mother to say, roughly and tender, here,
let me do it. Does one never grow-up into
all of a piece? One final hiccup and it's over.

Step out into dark feeling the way by the smooth
of the car, the clutter of wood too useful to junk.

Soft rain in the wind. White threads in the light.
Ash-leaves splayed on the glitter of gravel,
the cold air lifting the hairs on the scalp.
The shiver of death going down to the roots.
The flesh still warm. The last breath steaming.
White smoke in the light. Soft rain in the wind.

Prakrit ad absurdum

for Roy Norman

And when the Holy One was gone,
His dreams, His gentle jokes,
His admonitions and His messages of hope,
they told them over, one by one,

and in the telling
little things were changed—
from tongue to tongue the thought deranged.
Mis-spelled, the stories scribed at last

in alien verse, in Holy Writ,
drift sideways down the long brown
tide of Time; upside-down,
side by side, strange derelicts—

There was a poor man once
Found God a chaffinch in his net
And ate Him whole
Just for a bet

And lived a week
On the small winnings
And died within the month
From lack of sleep.
The wing-beat
Of the swallowed God
Brings the guilty heart release.

Now pious scholars
purse the lips, heads bent,
heart puzzling
what the Master meant.

There was a poor man once
Caught God in a half-inch mesh
And held Him tight
And ate Him fresh

And lived for years
To speak of it
Though bleating once a month
In sleep
The finbeat
Of the eaten God
Lies heavy and is queasy meat.

Audience with the heads of the Kings of Judah

at Cluny

They have accomplished calm.
Detached from finery and bodies both
they rest their case— as brought
before them, others, once.

As others, summoned later,
hammered their imagined
greatness into stone.
Now, in this Sanctuary,

beyond the sly impertinence
of wind and rain, of hungry frost,
a strange authority remains.
Soon shall they speak,

commend, commute, condemn.
This one has closed his eyes.
This one is opening his mouth.
Regard his teeth.

He cannot see or hear or think.
His crown, his cranium both gone—
though at his dark unspoken breath
we are undone.

Almost missing the comet

On the wet air the beat of bells,
the smell of horse-manure and trodden grass,
the gentle bicker of the stream and, through the trees,
the Hollow Lady of our dreams trailing
her sniffed-at handkerchief.

Once clear of trees, through still thin cloud
is this a child with tucked-in skirts wiggling a-hoola-hoop?
Or do you hear a half-crown deftly spun on a tin-topped table
begin the final chittering down to heads or tails,
to win or lose?

On the wet air the beat of bells,
the too much light from neighbours' windows,
the television's cube of ice, there, in the warm glass of their lives—
the Sky at Night, the sky at night. The comet
that I almost missed.

We sit on our hands

We sit on our hands. We cannot clap.
We children, who have shouted for

the Fairy and the Wicked Witch
and swallowed greasepaint, rhyme and sweat,

now see the footlights flicker out,
the daylight slitting through the flats.

We cast the skin of make-believe,
forgetting nothing's real unless

it bumps the blood across the heart's
twin ventricles of joy and grief.

Mere molluscs now, in mortgaged shells,
we dig beneath our soft, warm bums

to find the little Plastic God
who points us where and tunes us in

to sitcom, soap and turn-off wars
and drops, into the mind's cheap drum,

the coloured balls of Lady Luck.
Left-overs in a styrene dish,

crumpled packaging to bin—
O, children lost in pixcelled woods,

no longer knowing hot from cold,
no longer knowing bad from good,

society does not exist.
Society does not exist.

For Joan

The heart of adamant, the will of steel,
the soul a shadowed amethyst—
all fought the wound that will not heal.

The colours that you wore revealed
an eye for beauty at its best;
the heart of adamant, the will of steel

beneath deep blues and mauves concealed—
but as we met and gravely kissed
you fought the wound that will not heal.

Taking your hand the grip was real,
so frail and yet a warrior's wrist;
a heart of adamant, a will of steel.

Your man was dying, grey and ill:
you dragged him from presumptuous mists
and fought the wound that would not heal

and clasped his life and nursed him whole.
You were a one. Few could resist
that heart of adamant, that will of steel.

May there be bluebell woods and fields
of flowers and spirit's rest
from heart of adamant and will of steel,
from Time, the wound that would not heal.

For Phyllis

Mahonia against a red brick wall
and gentians in the rockery edge

and your strong fingers tugging out a string
of tough felicia for us to try.

You really want the blue and this one's pink—
It roots before you blink. She eyes my face,

My greying curls. *Aren't you a bonny lad.*
My turn to put down roots, go pink.

Bet you're quite the ladies' man— what
are you going to have to drink ?

Now as you wait, no-nonsense still, to die,
I think how Peter must be polishing The Gate

and Michael at his sword play, Gabriel
looking to his curls. Will they be taken in

by this tall, homely, country lass
who looks as if she's come straight

from her ride, who blurts it out,
Is he— is Godfrey anywhere around?

A greenfinch

The door hangs wide in Summer heat.
Twin panes of toughened glass,
full-length, stood open in the sun.

comfortable clutter kindly room

A cooling breeze, a stunning thud:
a greenfinch lying where the brick
rightangles to the wide stone step.

comforting question what to drink

With all the tenderness of guilt
I pick him up. He blinks an eye.
To my relief, he's coming round.

comfortable habits not having to think

I think of when to throw him up
into the air. With hopeful thoughts
I cuddle him. I turn him round.

and you so frustrate so consumed

The other eye is dead and gone.
The neck broken, the beak still.
I lie him, cat-safe, on a wall.

with bitterness and grief

An hour goes by before I tuck him in
the big brown wheelie-bin, beneath
some fronds of artichoke.

it seems I love too little care too much

Nothing he did was wrong, or unintelligent.
He simply flew the line he'd flown before
summer opened its toughened door—

not loved enough, you zombie through

End not begun

End not begun
green without sun
sun without shade
day without light

look down

unprinted earth
under the feet

look up

the wind's dark sleeve
rubs out the stars.

Oocooks at dawn

for Roger

So quiet, you hear the light-bulb sing.
Two tones: a perfect fourth apart:
not restful this. An odd relief,
the shocking grinding of a car pell-mell
haphazarding the bend. Put down the pen.
Nothing to say not better left. Slide
down the pillow, write it out
below the belt of dreams.

Cuckoo alarm. A hand goes out
to turn it off. Fails. Returns. Again,
like Noah I send it off: it brings back light.
4.45. Somewhere, so close it could be in my head,
my *ruthless bird*, with scarce a pause,
oo-cooks the dawn. Outside, a morning
stiff with rain-washed may. Strange ambience:
a great herbaceous coral reef I jellyfish along.
Adrift beneath the unleaved ash, look up
through mist sponged-clean of other songs
and see her bounce her wicked purposes,
proclaim them, brash as any loud-mouthed van
warning the water's being turned-off, turned-off.
Two tones. Hypnotic— and yes, it takes
an act of will to break the spell, to yell

I see you, cuckoo-bird. Just bugger-off!

But not until I make as if to scale she breaks away,
a spitfire-ace of twist and climb, of dive and turn.
A field away her trancing song resumes.
I swim the flowers back to the house
and wet-leg up the bedroom stairs
to all self-righteous birds' applause.

Calling the missing

Though it makes very little sense,
sometimes I stand at the door and call
as you would for a loved and missing cat.
First thing or last thing I come to this,
dawn or dusk – or stepping down

into the tingling dew or the heady scent,
I stand on the path of old brick under the arch
quite still for a moment and open the flask
of the soul and offer it wide to the luminous dark
to let whatever will come in.

Nothing. I remain incomplete. Just me.
Left to my own devices, sometimes I take
myself down from the wall like an old banjo
unplayed for years and try to pick out
the tune I was, how the fingers go.

Does it work? Well no, not the act of will
or whim – yet lifting my boot to prise
a stone or deep in a maze of allowed expense
on the tax return or driving in traffic in heavy rain –
there, with a prickling of the skin, the beautiful pain.

1st January 2000

We are dancing the Mother out of the dark
We are dancing the Mother all decked in her finery
We are dancing her out to the beat of our hearts
Turning her, blindfold, all in her jewellery
Dancing the Mother, dancing the Mother
To the intricate, difficult drum of our dreams.

What now? says the mind, much
as a cat lets go of a crippled mouse
to watch it run.

You go to the corner, they say: you'll
know, when you're there, what it is,
what to do—

Last night we stood in the wind, as fire
ripped up from the trampled earth in a glorious
scream from Hell.

Shivering, we stood in the wind and saw,
christened with gold, the faces of kin and kith
from two thousand years.

There, at the corner, we stood and cheered.
What now, squeaks the cornered mouse, where to
with our trail of blood?

The soul never

remembers getting in, starting to drive,
or the reason for the journey,
or where it might arrive—
just this need to get in and get moving
out of the perfect void.

Soon gets the hang, more or less, of the body,
the pedals, the gears, the lights
and, for a while, it's happy
just following the winding night, loving
the sense of time passing—

Indeed, bits of the way seem familiar,
bits make the flesh go cold,
make it urgently want to pull over,
run off into woods or fields, knowing
this isn't an option—

recalling, sometimes, how the old one
would always run wild in the wet,
how quickly accidents happen—
one sideways glance at the sunset—
a careless soul can be trapped

and screaming, as the body begins to die—
and why was it taking this journey,
was this where it meant to arrive?
And here come the Angels of Mercy
with their lights, their cutting knives—